Ecclesiastes

CHASING THE WIND

TRUTHFORLIFE®

Truth For Life is the Bible teaching ministry of Alistair Begg and a trusted source of biblical truth.

Daily Program

Listen to Alistair Begg teach verse by verse through books of the Bible and explain how to live as a follower of Jesus on the daily program *Truth For Life*. Search for *Truth For Life* where you listen to podcasts or on YouTube, download our free mobile app from your app store, listen online at truthforlife.org, or find the program on your local radio station by visiting **truthforlife.org/stationfinder**.

Daily Devotional

Begin each day learning from the Bible by listening to a five-minute daily devotional by Alistair Begg. Search for *Truth For Life Daily Devotions* on YouTube or where you listen to podcasts. You can also listen by downloading our mobile app or at **truthforlife.org/devotionals**. If you prefer to read the daily devotional, subscribe to receive it as a free daily email at **truthforlife.org/lists**.

Sermon Library

Alistair Begg has been teaching the Bible for more than forty years. Search his extensive sermon library to find teaching through many books of the Bible and on a wide variety of Christian living topics at **truthforlife.org/sermons**.

Free and Low-Cost Study Materials

Find free study guides and high-quality books for just a few dollars at **truthforlife.org/store**. Truth For Life sells books and other teaching materials at cost so that price is never a barrier to anyone who wants to learn more about Jesus.

Contact Truth For Life

PO Box 398000 Cleveland, OH 44139

phone 1 (888) 588-7884 **email** letters@truthforlife.org **web** truthforlife.org

IN THE LORD JESUS CHRIST IS THE ANSWER TO ALL THE DEEPEST HEARTACHES, LONGINGS, AND ABERRATIONS OF THE HUMAN CONDITION.

Alistair Begg

VERSE BY VERSE

BIBLE STUDY SERIES

Ecclesiastes

CHASING THE WIND

with

ALISTAIR BEGG

Truth For Life, Cleveland, OH 44139
In partnership with New Growth Press, Greensboro, NC 27401

Cover: Truth For Life, Seth Finnegan; imagery from unsplash.com/@mahkeo
Interior Design/Typesetting: Truth For Life, Seth Finnegan

Print ISBN: 978-1-64507-578-3
Ebook ISBN: 978-1-64507-579-0

Printed in India

29 28 27 26 25 1 2 3 4 5

TABLE OF CONTENTS

VERSE BY VERSE

Bible Study Series

The Verse by Verse Bible study series is inspired by Alistair Begg's decades-long pattern of and passion for expository preaching. The aim of these studies is no different than the mission of Truth For Life: to teach the Bible with clarity and relevance so that unbelievers will be converted, believers will be established, and local churches will be strengthened. Each of those three facets can be realized only because God's Word is "living and active" (Heb. 4:12); indeed, it is a seed meant to be sown in order that it might fall into good soil, grow, and yield much fruit (Luke 8:4–15).

The great inherent danger when we study the Bible is that we want to move immediately from our reading of the biblical text to personal application. To combat that temptation, each session in this volume follows the following structure, which will help you spend adequate time meditating on and studying each passage before attempting to apply it to your own life:

Open the Book — Read the passage in view, observing key themes, verses, or questions that arise from the text.

Study the Book — Using commentary from Alistair Begg, consider the passage's meaning in its context by answering questions and making theological connections.

Live Out the Book — Respond to God's Word in faith and repentance, applying its principles to particular areas of life.

Praise and Prayer — Use the provided prompts to turn the truths learned into praise and prayer, thank God for His love, confess sins, and go forth to serve Him with joy.

Further Study *(Optional)* — Supplement the session's content with related Bible passages and additional resources.

To reinforce good Bible reading habits, the questions in the **Study the Book** and **Live Out the Book** sections follow a basic progression from *interpretation* to *application*. Each session adapts the same set of four questions to pertain specifically to the biblical passage in view. These are:

- What is the main point of this portion?
- What does God—Father, Son, or Holy Spirit—reveal of Himself?
- What insight am I given into myself and into my life situation? Is there an example of a warning to heed? A promise to claim?
- What does Christ require of me now, in thought, word, or action?[1]

[1] Used with permission from Scripture Union. https://scriptureunion.org/how-to-read-pray/.

Tips for Individuals

- Follow the provided Reading Plan in the Introduction to maximize comprehension of the material.
- Read or listen to the entire biblical book in a single sitting prior to beginning the study to familiarize yourself with its structure and themes. For Ecclesiastes, this should take around thirty minutes.
- Use a good study Bible for reference as you work through the content.
- For each session, aim to memorize at least one key verse.
- Share what you learn with others as you progress to solidify your knowledge and application of the material and to encourage someone else.

Tips for Groups

- Come to the meeting prepared, with participants having read the Scripture, familiarized themselves with the content, and completed the **Open** and **Study** sections.
- Read the passage for each session out loud together as a group, breaking it into smaller sections for several people to read.
- Spend most of your discussion time in the **Live Out** section, working through the questions together and using the **Study** content for reference. Take liberties to emphasize a particular question or two if it lends itself to greater discussion in the group.
- Utilize the **Praise and Prayer** section to share personal requests with the group, committing to pray for one another throughout the week.
- Consider asking your pastor for insight on any difficult questions or themes that arise during the study.
- Studies in this series are typically arranged in twelve or twenty-four sessions so that they work well for those who meet weekly, biweekly, or even monthly.

Leading a group through this study? See Appendix A for additional tips.

Before you begin, ponder this reality: Of all the places you could be, among all the circumstances that you could be facing, God has providentially ordered your steps in order that you would open up this study, search the Scriptures, and hear from God Himself through His Word.

MAKE THE BOOK LIVE TO ME, O LORD,
SHOW ME THYSELF WITHIN THY WORD,
SHOW ME MYSELF AND SHOW ME MY SAVIOR,
AND MAKE THE BOOK LIVE TO ME.

R. Hudson Pope, "Make the Book Live to Me"

INTRODUCTION

ECCLESIASTES: CHASING THE WIND

"The words of the wise are like goads, and like nails firmly fixed are the collected sayings; they are given by one Shepherd." ***—Ecclesiastes 12:11***

Trapped in a dark world without a clear a view of God, the writer of Ecclesiastes sought frantically for some light on the path—but indulging in everything this world had to offer left him empty and unfulfilled. After climbing high on life's ladder, he made the tragic discovery that it was propped against the wrong wall. Cynical about worldly achievements, he began to question—rightly—whether anything mattered or everything was only vanity.

In this study, we'll consider what this challenging and relevant Old Testament meditation has to say about life's apparent futility and will be reminded that there is only one true hope that can give our existence lasting meaning. When so many pass their days running down dead-end streets, we can live with purpose. First, though, we must discover and embrace what it means to fear God, which is the beginning of true wisdom.

Key Themes

- the vanity of life
- fear of God
- effects of the fall
- toil and labor
- enjoyment of God's creation

Setting

Likely written sometime during the period of Israel's monarchy (900–576 BC), Ecclesiastes addresses a diverse group of Israelite God-fearers—people with backgrounds as royal counselors and day laborers alike (Eccl. 8:1–9; 11:6). The book calls God's people to heed wisdom and fear their Creator (Eccl. 12:9–14).

Characters

The Preacher: The title given to the author of Ecclesiastes (1:1). The Hebrew word translated into English as "the Preacher" is *Qoheleth*, from the Hebrew verb *qahal*, which means "to assemble." It suggests the picture of a respected Israelite king standing before an assembly of his people, instructing them in wisdom. Ecclesiastes reveals that the Preacher was a Davidic king (1:1), was greatly wise and wealthy (1:12–2:11), and arranged many proverbs (12:9). Though the book is technically anonymous, Solomon best fits the description.

Words/Phrases/Definitions

Vanity: Translated from the Hebrew word *hevel*, it literally means a "mist" or "vapor." It is used throughout Ecclesiastes in this sense but can also refer figuratively to something that is transient, fleeting, or elusive—an enigma or paradox.

Under the Sun: In the Preacher's view, this phrase refers to the time and the place in which life occurs. Ecclesiastes is written not from the vantage point of the infinite, personal creator God but from that of His creation.

Fear God: This repeated phrase refers to the heart disposition of God's children before Him—one not of terror but of reverential awe in response to God's character.

READING PLAN

WEEK	PRIMARY TEXT
1	Ecclesiastes 1
2	Ecclesiastes 2
3	Ecclesiastes 3
4	Ecclesiastes 4
5	Ecclesiastes 5:1–7
6	Ecclesiastes 5:8–6:12
7	Ecclesiastes 7
8	Ecclesiastes 8–9
9	Ecclesiastes 10
10	Ecclesiastes 11
11	Ecclesiastes 12:1–8
12	Ecclesiastes 12:9–14

SESSION ONE

ECCLESIASTES 1

A WORD TO THE WISE

"I have seen everything that is done under the sun, and behold, all is vanity and a striving after wind." ***—Ecclesiastes 1:14***

Open the Book

Go to the Lord in prayer, asking Him to help you understand and receive His Word. Then read Ecclesiastes 1.

In a sentence or two, summarize what this passage says. (For this response, focus on understanding what the words themselves communicate. Don't move yet to application.)

What literary features are present in this passage? (Look for repeated words, contrasts, metaphors, questions and answers, illustrations, and references or allusions to other parts of Scripture.)

What lingering questions do you have?

Study the Book

T. S. Eliot once remarked, "Human kind / Cannot bear very much reality."[2] What we find throughout Ecclesiastes, however, is a heavy dose of just that: reality.

In most of our twenty-first-century cultures, entertainment takes us to worlds of fantasy and mirage, to that which is out and beyond us. We falsely believe that if we could only get out of *our* reality, then perhaps we could find the answers. But the book of Ecclesiastes provides us no such escape. Instead, this ancient meditation continues generation after generation to shine its searchlight on matters of real life.

Verse 1 introduces us to the Preacher. He does in writing what few people are willing to do even in their minds: He wrestles with the enigmas of life, searching tirelessly for answers. The Preacher doesn't approach his subject like a distanced university professor, raising questions only to watch his students debate one another. Rather, he's involved in the very questions he raises. He has built an observation tower at ground level, so to speak.

Who was "the Preacher"?

The Preacher (also known as "the Teacher" or "Qoheleth" in other translations) introduces himself here in verse 1 as "the son of David, king in Jerusalem." Although he doesn't actually say, "I am Solomon," Solomon best fits the description.

[2] T. S. Eliot, "Burnt Norton," *Four Quartets* (1943).

What does the Preacher observe? Our answer is in **verse 2**, which reads more like a conclusion than an introduction: "All is vanity." In Hebrew writing, it was customary to put the most important point up front. The Preacher follows this pattern, piquing our curiosity right away: *How can he say that everything is vanity?* It's an invitation to read on to learn how the Preacher arrived at such a conclusion—and whether his insights will persuade us of the same.

The Preacher points out in **verse 3** that his survey of life "under the sun" is conducted not from God's vantage point but from man's. The Preacher will show us that in any framework that fails to account for God's existence, everything under the sun, from birth to death, is meaningless.

In **verses 3–18**, the Preacher unpacks his conclusion in six points:

1. *Life is marked by drudgery.* Again, in **verse 3**, the Preacher asks, "What does man gain by all the toil at which he toils under the sun?" Put simply: Life can be boring! It doesn't matter our vocation; for everyone—mothers at home, college students, CEOs, retirees—much of life possesses an inherent monotony.

2. *Life is marked by transience.* In **verse 4**, the Preacher's observation of generations coming and going testifies to our lives' frailty and brevity. As our days go by and familiar faces pass away, the words of Psalm 90:10 seem to resonate with us: "The years of our life are seventy, or even by reason of strength eighty; ... they are soon gone, and we fly away."

3. *Life is repetitive.* The Preacher observes in **verses 5–7** several features of our natural world: the sun, wind, and streams. The sun, he points out, is in its same course every day; it never goes on vacation. The wind may blow somebody's hat off, provide a refreshing breeze, or make the aircraft bounce around—but it doesn't cease. Streams flow into the sea, yet the sea is never full. The Preacher wants us to see that our human experience closely mirrors the natural world. Life is repetitive.

4. *Life is insatiable.* As **verse 8** says, "All things are full of weariness; a man cannot utter it; the eye is not satisfied with seeing, nor the ear filled with hearing." In other words, life has an appetite that can never be satisfied.

5. *Life is the same old, same old.* "What has been is what will be, and what has been done is what will be done, and there is nothing new under the sun. ... It has been already in the ages before us" **(vv. 9–10)**. Just when we think we've had a new idea, we discover it's already been done. In the framework of life "under the sun," there are no surprises; there are no true breakthroughs.

6. *Life is marked by insignificance.* In **verses 12–18**, the Preacher raises for us an essential question: Is there true life before death, or are we limited to mere survival? While king in Jerusalem, he saw everything done under the sun, concluding that it was merely a striving after the wind. "What is crooked cannot be made straight," he says, "and what is lacking cannot be counted" **(v. 15)**. Life is like a Rubik's Cube with two blocks missing: No matter how many times we spin it, it can't be solved, because it's inherently flawed.

The Preacher concludes chapter 1 with **verses 16–18**, which tell us that in his intellectual pursuits of wisdom, madness, and folly, he wound up vexed and sorrowful. This, too, he discerned, is a striving after the wind.

In two or three sentences, summarize the main point of this passage. How does it fit into the broader picture of God's revelation?

Life "under the sun" apart from God is ultimately meaningless. But for those asking, "Is there life before death?" there is the promise of Jesus, which came centuries after Ecclesiastes: "I am the way, and the truth, and *the life*" (John 14:6, emphasis added). We know today what it would take the Preacher eleven more chapters to discover in part: that in the Lord Jesus Christ is the answer to all the deepest heartaches and greatest longings we experience. In order to fully appreciate that fact's implications, however, we must first come to terms with the vanity of life apart from Him.

God does not appear as a character in Ecclesiastes 1, but we may be reminded of Him as we think of the vanity the Preacher describes. How does God stand in contrast to what we see here?

Of the six points the Preacher makes, which are most relevant to your life situation? Are any of them particularly hard for you to believe? Why?

Jesus offers us a significance and permanence that the world cannot. Are there any worldly promises that you tend to put your hope in? How might you lay those at the feet of Christ?

♪

Praise and Prayer

USE PSALM 90:9–17 FOR PRAISE AND MEDITATION:

For all our days pass away under your wrath;
we bring our years to an end like a sigh.
The years of our life are seventy,
or even by reason of strength eighty;
yet their span is but toil and trouble;
they are soon gone, and we fly away.
Who considers the power of your anger,
and your wrath according to the fear of you?
So teach us to number our days
that we may get a heart of wisdom.
Return, O LORD! How long?
Have pity on your servants!
Satisfy us in the morning with your steadfast love,
that we may rejoice and be glad all our days.
Make us glad for as many days as you have afflicted us,
and for as many years as we have seen evil.
Let your work be shown to your servants,
and your glorious power to their children.
Let the favor of the Lord our God be upon us,
and establish the work of our hands upon us;
yes, establish the work of our hands!

Praise and Prayer

USE THE TRUTHS LEARNED FOR PERSONAL PRAYER:

- **Thank** the Lord for showing you the emptiness of life apart from Him.
- **Repent** of your tendency to search for fulfillment apart from God Himself.
- **Ask** God to satisfy the longings of your heart through His Word and presence.
- **Ask** for Christ's wisdom as you strive to honor Him in a life marked by drudgery.

Further Study

- **Related passages:** 1 Kings 4:29–34; Psalm 90:10–14.
- **Related sermon:** "A Word to the Wise"
- **Related article:** "Is There Life Before Death?"

Scan the QR code to find links to the additional resources, or visit tfl.org/ecclesiastes-list.

SESSION TWO

ECCLESIASTES 2

THE SEARCH FOR SATISFACTION

"There is nothing better for a person than that he should eat and drink and find enjoyment in his toil. This also, I saw, is from the hand of God, for apart from him who can eat or who can have enjoyment?" ***—Ecclesiastes 2:24–25***

Open the Book

Go to the Lord in prayer, asking Him to help you understand and receive His Word. Then read Ecclesiastes 2.

In a sentence or two, summarize what this passage says. (For this response, focus on understanding what the words themselves communicate. Don't move yet to application.)

What literary features are present in this passage? (Look for repeated words, contrasts, metaphors, questions and answers, illustrations, and references or allusions to other parts of Scripture.)

What lingering questions do you have?

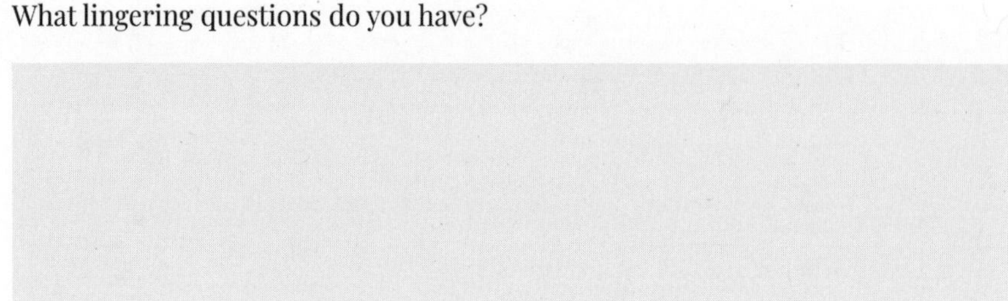

Study the Book

Ecclesiastes 2 focuses on the Preacher's search for satisfaction. Having acknowledged in chapter 1 that the way of wisdom doesn't hold the answer to life's questions, he now considers the path of pleasure: "I said in my heart, 'Come now, I will test you with pleasure; enjoy yourself'" **(v. 1)**. But this path also proves meaningless. He concludes the chapter with the familiar phrase: "This also is vanity" **(v. 26)**.

As the Preacher recounts his travels on the path of pleasure, he highlights five routes that wound up being dead-end streets, along with three concluding observations.

The Preacher's Five Routes

First is *the route of laughter* in **verse 2**: "I said of laughter, 'It is mad,' and of pleasure, 'What use is it?'" It's said that laughter is medicine for the soul, but the Preacher says it's foolish. He means to show that laughter is light, fleeting, and superficial. It's like contrasting a comedy show with a tragedy play: The former is a flash in the pan, while the latter, because of its weightiness, may remain in our memories for years. Consequently, the Preacher views laughter as mere folly.

Second, we see *the route of wine* in **verse 3**: "I searched with my heart how to cheer my body with wine." The Preacher isn't commenting on the merits or demerits of abstaining from alcohol. Rather, he's addressing the futility of using alcohol as a drug to mask one's unsatisfied, soul-level longings. Even a moderated use of alcohol proves fruitless in the end, from the Preacher's vantage point, for he says he partook of wine with "my heart still guiding me with wisdom" **(v. 3)**.

Third, there's *the route of achievement* in **verses 4–6**. The Preacher describes the various building projects he undertook: houses, vineyards, gardens, parks, fruit trees, and reservoirs to water his forests. But in the end, all of his contributions still left him feeling empty.

Fourth, the Preacher takes us with him down *the route of influence* in **verses 7–9**. He boasts of the number of people working for him and all his great possessions—herds, flocks, silver, gold, the treasures of kings and provinces, singers, and all the delights of a person's heart. The outcome? "I became great," writes the Preacher, "and surpassed all who were before me in Jerusalem" **(v. 9)**. Yet still it was not enough to provide lasting satisfaction.

Finally, the Preacher recounts *the route of indulgence* in **verses 10–11**. He indulged in whatever he desired, resisting no prospect of outward entertainment or inward satisfaction. Yet still, having taken an account of all he had done, he found it was all vanity **(v. 11)**.

The Preacher's Three Observations

In verses **12–17**, the Preacher observes the vanity of wise living. Though in some sense there's more gain in worldly wisdom than in folly, we have to temper our expectations—after all, "The wise dies just like the fool!" **(v. 16)**. The Preacher then observes the vanity of toil in **verses 18–23**. Under the sun, he contends, "I hated all my toil" **(v. 18)**. He isn't saying that work, where God is in control, is irrelevant, but he *is* pointing out that when our labor is an end in itself, our days will be filled with sorrow **(v. 23)**. From man's perspective under the sun, his work is vanity.

In **verses 24–26**, though, we find a hint of hope: "There is nothing better for a person than that he should eat and drink and find enjoyment in his toil" **(v. 24)**. Simply put, there are two foundations upon which we can build our lives: upon sand—the way of folly—or upon the rock, leading to true satisfaction (Matt. 7:24–27). When we understand the true and living God and why He sent Christ, enjoyment of all the gifts of which the Preacher speaks becomes an attractive proposition.

In two or three sentences, summarize the main point of this passage. How does it fit into the broader picture of God's revelation?

Live Out the Book

At one point or another, all of us have heard calls to venture down these dead-end streets in search of fulfillment. But the only solid joys and lasting treasures we may discover are those that are found in a personal, living faith in God. In giving us the book of Ecclesiastes, God warns us, "Careful! Don't go down these dead-end streets! Instead, trust My Son." We must choose today whom we'll serve. Will we search for satisfaction down life's aimless alleyways? Or will we learn from the Preacher's mistakes and instead meet God at the crossroads in the person of His Son?

Psalm 16:11 speaks of pleasures that come only from God's hand. How do these differ from those the Preacher sought in chapter 2? How can we obtain them?

What experience do you have with any of the five "dead-end streets" the Preacher identifies in Ecclesiastes 2:1–11? How did they leave you unsatisfied?

How does faith in God's Son transform our ability to truly enjoy life?

♪

Praise and Prayer

USE THE FOLLOWING HYMN FOR PRAISE AND MEDITATION:

Be Thou my vision, O Lord of my heart;
Naught be all else to me save that Thou art;
Thou my best thought, by day or by night,
Waking or sleeping, Thy presence my light.

Be Thou my wisdom and Thou my true word,
I ever with Thee and Thou with me, Lord,
Thou my great Father, I Thy true son,
Thou in me dwelling and I with Thee one.

Be Thou my battle shield, sword for the fight;
Be Thou my dignity, Thou my delight,
Thou my soul's shelter, Thou my high tower;
Raise Thou me heavenward, O power of my power.

Riches I heed not nor man's empty praise;
Thou mine inheritance, now and always,
Thou and Thou only, first in my heart;
High King of heaven, my treasure Thou art.

High King of heaven, my victory won,
May I reach heaven's joys, O bright heaven's sun!
Heart of my own heart, whatever befall,
Still be my vision, O Ruler of all.

**"Be Thou My Vision" trans. Mary E. Byrne,
versified by Eleanor Hull**

Praise and Prayer

USE THE TRUTHS LEARNED FOR PERSONAL PRAYER:

- **Praise** God for mercifully showing you the ultimate futility of resting in fleeting things.
- **Confess** to the Lord regarding any dead-end streets you have walked down, **repent** of any accompanying sins, and **pray** the Lord will help you avoid them moving forward.
- **Ask** God to lead you into a deeper understanding of Jesus' finished and ongoing work on your behalf.

Further Study

- **Related passages:** Psalm 16:1–11; Matthew 7:24–27
- **Related sermon:** "The Search for Satisfaction"
- **Related devotion:** "Nothing Can Satisfy" by Charles Spurgeon

Scan the QR code to find links to the additional resources, or visit tfl.org/ecclesiastes-list.

SESSION THREE

ECCLESIASTES 3

ETERNITY ON MY MIND

"He has made everything beautiful in its time. Also, he has put eternity into man's heart." ***—Ecclesiastes 3:11***

Open the Book

Go to the Lord in prayer, asking Him to help you understand and receive His Word. Then read Ecclesiastes 3.

In a sentence or two, summarize what this passage says. (For this response, focus on understanding what the words themselves communicate. Don't move yet to application.)

What literary features are present in this passage? (Look for repeated words, contrasts, metaphors, questions and answers, illustrations, and references or allusions to other parts of Scripture.)

What lingering questions do you have?

Study the Book

Ecclesiastes reveals that as creatures of time, we were made for eternity. We were made for God's presence. Consequently, when we turn away from God, we shouldn't be surprised if frustration and confusion soon follow. The Preacher turns to these matters in chapter 3.

The Same Old Routine

Verses 1–8 are a description of the cycle of life: "For everything there is a season, and a time for every matter under heaven" **(v. 1)**. These verses contain twenty-eight statements, all to make this point: Life involves the repeating of the same old routine, over which we have no lasting control. This cycle confronts us. In the grand scheme of our relatively short lives, we can only see a fraction of time's movement. As we try to make sense of our part in the vastness of time, we realize that it's tremendously insignificant.

A Whole New Perspective

This dose of reality brings us to **verse 9**: "What gain has the worker from his toil?" This isn't a financial question; it's more foundational than that. The Preacher essentially says, "What's the point of going to work? To buy food so that we can stay alive, just to go back to work for more money to buy food—and the cycle repeats." But there's a better perspective: "I have seen the business that God has given to the children of man to be busy with" **(v. 10)**. The frustration we experience, in other words, is a God-given burden.

What does this reality point to? The answer is in **verse 11**: "He has made everything beautiful in its time. Also, he has put eternity into man's heart, yet so that he cannot find out what God has done from the beginning to the end." With these words, the Preacher introduces a new perspective from which to deal with life's cyclical drudgery. In essence, he is teaching (or reminding) readers that God created a pristine world that is full of beauty. He set it in time and space. God then made men and women that they may know Him, enjoying all the benefits of divine companionship.

Neither death nor frustration were designed into that system. But humanity turned its back on all that God had to say. As a result, the notion of eternity in our hearts is actually something that tyrannizes. We're tormented by the cycles of futility, frustrated by a sense of homesickness we can't explain.

This is the burden alluded to in **verse 10**. God has put eternity in our hearts **(v. 11)**. We have been made for His pleasure, created in His image. Therefore, we'll always be dissatisfied until we come to know and commune with Him. Once aware of this burden, we can cry to Him for help and reach the solution.

The Possibility of a Solid Conviction

How we respond to this cycle of life reveals a great deal about us. The person who trusts God can accept the program described in this chapter as a God-given gift rather than a burden. This is the point of **verses 12–13**. Eating, drinking, taking pleasure in all our toils—these are God's gifts to man. For the unbeliever, they eventually prove to be absolutely meaninglessness. But for the believer, even the most monotonous job can be done to God's glory! The mundane becomes magnificent in God's plan.

The Preacher finally settles with his finitude in **verses 14–15**. He knows that he, like the rest of us, will pass through the cycle of life—but he's fine with it, because he knows that God's works and purposes endure forever **(v. 14)**. His significance is ultimately not in himself but in his identity in God. This is true for all believers. We were made for God's pleasure. We exist for someone other than ourselves. When we're brought to this perspective, our entire worldview changes.

The Reality of Injustice

Verses 16–17 then offer a troubling observation: "In the place of justice, even there was wickedness, and in the place of righteousness, even there was wickedness." The Preacher confronts the harsh reality that injustice and wickedness often prevail where justice and righteousness ought to reign. This stark truth can lead to feelings of despair and questioning of God's sovereignty. Yet the Preacher reassures us that God will judge both the righteous and the wicked, affirming that perfect justice will ultimately prevail and providing hope that despite the prevalence of injustice, God's perfect judgment will come in His timing.

The Fate of Creation

In **verses 18–21**, the Preacher reflects on the common fate of humans and animals. His comparison emphasizes the mortality and frailty of human life. Despite our intellect and achievements, we share the same end as beasts, returning to dust. Isn't it humbling and sobering to reflect on this shared destiny and on the mystery surrounding life after death? And yet even these ponderings from the Preacher can (and should!) lead to a deeper appreciation of life and a recognition of our dependence on God for now and forever.

Finding Joy in the Present

Finally, **verse 22** concludes with a practical encouragement: "I saw that there is nothing better than that a man should rejoice in his work, for that is his lot. Who can bring him to see what will be after him?" Contentment and joy truly are rare jewels. Finding them in the present, despite life's uncertainties and injustices, is a goal to be pursued and a gift to be cherished. While we may not understand all of God's plans, we can trust Him and find fulfillment in all He has set or will set on our paths.

In two or three sentences, summarize the main point of this passage. How does it fit into the broader picture of God's revelation?

Live Out the Book

We were made for eternity. God has created us for a purpose—but unless we fulfill that divine purpose, we'll never be fully satisfied with what is offered along life's journey. We have a restlessness in our lives that God has laid on us, so that when we face up to it, He, the Burden-Maker, may become to us the Burden-Taker.

The Preacher states that God has put eternity into our hearts (Eccl. 3:11). Why did God do this? How does it serve to bring Him glory through us?

Do you tend to view the monotony of life described in Ecclesiastes 3:1–9 as drudgery or delight? What is the key to achieving the latter perspective?

In Matthew 10:29, Jesus speaks of the Father's providential care for His children. In what areas of your life have you lacked faith in Christ's promise? How might you bring ongoing burdens to Him even now?

Praise and Prayer

USE THIS EXCERPT FROM MATTHEW HENRY'S COMMENTARY FOR PRAISE AND MEDITATION:

There is a wonderful harmony in the divine Providence and all its disposals, so that the events of it, when they come to be considered in their relations and tendencies, together with the seasons of them, will appear very beautiful, to the glory of God and the comfort of those that trust in him. Though we see not the complete beauty of Providence, yet we shall see it, and a glorious sight it will be, when the mystery of God shall be finished. Then every thing shall appear to have been done in the most proper time and it will be the wonder of eternity.

Praise and Prayer

USE THE TRUTHS LEARNED FOR PERSONAL PRAYER:

- **Prayerfully reflect** upon this season of your life.
- **Ask** the Holy Spirit to reveal His will for you at present.
- **Ask** God to assure you of your identity in Him.
- **Praise** the Lord for placing the realities of eternity into your heart.

Further Study

- **Related passages:** Matthew 10:29; Romans 1:19–23
- **Related sermon:** “Eternity on My Mind”
- **Related devotion:** “A God-Given Burden”

Scan the QR code to find links to the additional resources, or visit tfl.org/ecclesiastes-list.

SESSION FOUR

ECCLESIASTES 4

ALL THOSE LONELY PEOPLE

"Two are better than one, because they have a good reward for their toil."
—Ecclesiastes 4:9

Open the Book

Go to the Lord in prayer, asking Him to help you understand and receive His Word. Then read Ecclesiastes 4.

In a sentence or two, summarize what this passage says. (For this response, focus on understanding what the words themselves communicate. Don't move yet to application.)

What literary features are present in this passage? (Look for repeated words, contrasts, metaphors, questions and answers, illustrations, and references or allusions to other parts of Scripture.)

What lingering questions do you have?

Study the Book

Ecclesiastes 4 deals with the topic of loneliness. **Verse 1** contains the Preacher's observation that "the oppressed ... had no one to comfort them!" In **verse 8**, he describes a person who has no companion—not even a son or brother. And **verses 13–16** envision a scenario in which a foolish king transfers his rule to an upstart youth, producing discontinuity in his kingdom. No comforter **(v. 1)**, no companion **(v. 8)**, and no continuity **(vv. 13–16)**—the word that comes to mind is *lonely*, a word that defines far too many in our world.

The Preacher invites us to analyze the condition of loneliness from four angles.

"Give Me Death"

Though blunt, the Preacher's message in **verses 1–3** is simply "You're better off dead." **Verse 1** begins, "Again I saw all the oppressions that are done under the sun. And behold, the tears of the oppressed, and they had no one to comfort them!" In the world, power is on the side of the oppressor, and few step in to help the oppressed. This leads to the Preacher thinking "the dead ... more fortunate than the living" **(v. 2)**. Taking it one step further, he concludes it would be better for us to have never been born **(v. 3)**. Such oppression under the sun—that is, apart from God—makes for a miserable existence.

Three Bad Ends

The message of **verses 4–6** can be summarized with three words: *envy, poverty,* and *anxiety*.

In **verse 4**, the Preacher, observing laborers, concludes that the motivation in much of our work is a desire to outshine those around us. The wheel of life is driven by a competitive spirit. When our motive is to keep up with the Joneses, we will never be satisfied, for Mr. and Mrs. Jones are always at least a step ahead of us. In our search for satisfaction, our reach will always exceed our grasp.

Not only is envy futile, but poverty is also. **Verse 5** pictures a lazy individual, idleness eating away at what he has and what he is. Impoverished, he watches as his indolence erodes his self-control, his grasp of reality, his capacity to care, and even his self-respect.

What is the remedy to the two extremes of envy and poverty? **Verse 6** points out the answer: "Better is a handful of quietness than two hands full of toil and a striving after wind." In other words, it's better to have modest earnings and a restful mind than to have large gains and an anxious soul. It's a matter of contentment.

A House Too Large for One

Verses 7–8 then paint an all too familiar picture: "Again, I saw vanity under the sun: one person who has no other, either son or brother, yet there is no end to all his toil, and his eyes are never satisfied with riches, so that he never asks, 'For whom am I toiling and depriving myself of pleasure?' This also is vanity and an unhappy business."

It's a commentary on life in many wealthy countries today, isn't it? A beautiful home set in the midst of acreage, filled with all sorts of entertainment and amenities—yet in this lovely home lives a man all on his own. He never planned to be on his own. He didn't build the house for himself. And here he's described in Ecclesiastes 4: "no end to all his toil" **(v. 8)**.

Alone on the Throne

We may summarize **verses 13–16** in a phrase: *It's lonely at the top*. The Preacher describes a poor, wise youth and an old, foolish king. In his account, the king grows old and crusty, too long in the saddle. It seems he's overstayed his welcome on the throne. Then the wise youth rises up, loved by all, and ascends from poverty to kingship. But over time, we might imagine, the people criticize him as they did his predecessor; the crowds dwindle, and he, too, is succeeded by a yet younger, fitter king. He is unappreciated or, worse yet, forgotten entirely.

Today, whether in corporate life, local churches, or some other establishment, successors come and go at the phrase "We are going in a new direction." It's lonely at the top.

In two or three sentences, summarize the main point of this passage. How does it fit into the broader picture of God's revelation?

Live Out the Book

What can relieve the loneliness the Preacher describes in chapter 4? **Verse 9** affirms, "Two are better than one"—better for work, better for keeping warm, better for prevailing overall. But even then, there's not a person on earth who can meet our deepest need.

Who can meet that need in us? Paul gives us the solution in Ephesians 2:12–13: "Remember that you were ... separated from Christ, alienated from the commonwealth of Israel and strangers to the covenants of promise, having no hope and without God in the world." That is true loneliness. But by the Gospel has come a radical transformation: "Now in Christ Jesus you who once were far off have been brought near by the blood of Christ."

Paul's words are an invitation for the lonely to be welcomed into Christ's embrace. God has come to us, seeking us out like a shepherd seeks his lost sheep. In Christ, we have the prospect of a constant companionship to remedy our lonely conditions.

How does knowing God inform how we view evils like oppression, envy, poverty, anxiety, discontentment, and loneliness?

How have you struggled with the idol of comparison? How can you cultivate Christian contentment?

How does belonging to Christ's body, the church, help alleviate the Christian's loneliness? Who is one person you know who seems lonely? How might you be able to help?

♪

Praise and Prayer

USE THE FOLLOWING HYMN FOR PRAISE AND MEDITATION:

What a friend we have in Jesus,
All our sins and griefs to bear!
What a privilege to carry
Everything to God in prayer!
Oh, what peace we often forfeit,
Oh, what needless pain we bear,
All because we do not carry
Everything to God in prayer!

Have we trials and temptations?
Is there trouble anywhere?
We should never be discouraged;
Take it to the Lord in prayer!
Can we find a friend so faithful
Who will all our sorrows share?
Jesus knows our every weakness;
Take it to the Lord in prayer!

Are we weak and heavy laden,
Cumbered with a load of care?
Precious Savior, still our refuge—
Take it to the Lord in prayer!
Do your friends despise, forsake you?
Take it to the Lord in prayer!
In His arms He'll take and shield you;
You will find a solace there.

"What a Friend We Have in Jesus"
by Joseph Scriven

Praise and Prayer

USE THE TRUTHS LEARNED FOR PERSONAL PRAYER:

- **Ask** the Holy Spirit to search your heart, exposing the areas of your life in which you lack peace and contentment.
- **Pray** that your local church leaders would find comfort and joy in their relationship with Christ.
- **Pray** for those people in your life who live without regard for God.

Further Study

- **Related passages:** Isaiah 55:1–9; John 3:16–17
- **Related sermon:** “All Those Lonely People”
- **Related devotion:** “The Lie of Isolation”

Scan the QR code to find links to the additional resources, or visit tfl.org/ecclesiastes-list.

SESSION FIVE

ECCLESIASTES 5:1–7

CONCERNING WORSHIP

"When dreams increase and words grow many, there is vanity; but God is the one you must fear." ***—Ecclesiastes 5:7***

Open the Book

Go to the Lord in prayer, asking Him to help you understand and receive His Word. Then read Ecclesiastes 5:1–7.

In a sentence or two, summarize what this passage says. (For this response, focus on understanding what the words themselves communicate. Don't move yet to application.)

What literary features are present in this passage? (Look for repeated words, contrasts, metaphors, questions and answers, illustrations, and references or allusions to other parts of Scripture.)

What lingering questions do you have?

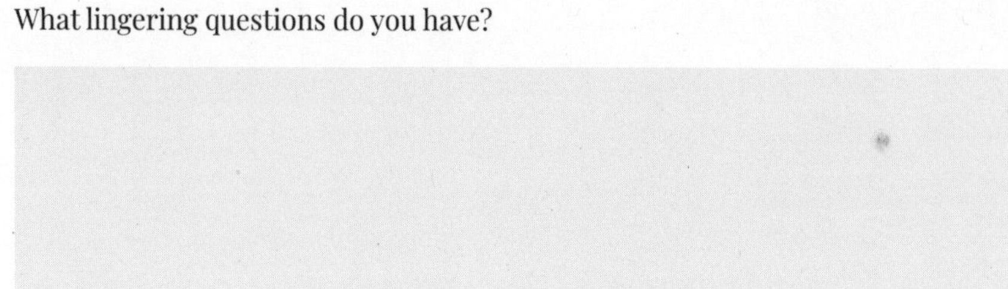

Study the Book

The opening verses of Ecclesiastes 5 deal with the matter of proper worship. Having gone down various avenues in search of meaning (chapters 1–4), the Preacher then paused to observe Israel's worship. As he watched the comings and goings of God's people to the place of worship, it became apparent that all was not well. Corruption had crept into those who professed faith, causing confusion about whom they were worshipping and how He was to be worshipped.

We might say this portion of Ecclesiastes is addressed to the nominal churchgoer—the person who knows a number of the songs, taps along to the tunes, listens to the sermons with half an ear, remembers very little of what he hears, and rarely responds to God's internal working with obedience. Concerning worship, the Preacher issues four instructions.

Guard Your Steps

Verse 1 contains the first instruction: "Guard your steps when you go to the house of God." We may think of Psalm 34:3: "Oh, magnify the LORD with me, and let us exalt his name together!" This is our aim when we come to worship. Unfortunately, few of us prepare for the task. Preparing for worship—guarding our steps—is crucial if we are to be true worshippers. We must be spiritually alive, spiritually assisted, and spiritually active in how we prepare ourselves for worship.

Watch Your Mouth

In **verses 2–3**, the Preacher warns against meaningless, mechanical worship. "Be not rash with your mouth," he cautions **(v. 2)**, adding in **verse 3** that speaking excessively will inevitably lead to us saying nonsense. Attempting to impress those around us, we'll dribble our religious clichés in prayer. Instead, we would do well to quietly consider the infinite qualitative distinction between God and ourselves **(v. 2)**. When God looks at us as worshippers, He listens not through the speakers, as it were, but through the stethoscope. He hears what's really happening on the inside, irrespective of the ambient noise—the things we want to present to the outside.

Keep Your Vows

The Preacher next addresses the issue of vowing before God: "When you vow a vow to God," he warns, "do not delay in paying it" **(v. 4)**. Vowing to God in worship presents us with a danger. We come to worship, God's Word speaks to us, and as a result, we tell God we'll do something in response. "It is better that you should not vow," the Preacher states in **verse 5**. But if we do speak in this manner to God, then we ought to be careful to fulfill our oath, lest we deny that we spoke it in the first place and increase our sin **(v. 6)**.

Stand in Awe

Verse 7 features the final instruction concerning worship: "God is the one you must fear." In other words, we are to stand in awe of God. *Awe* is a synonym for reverential fear, not terror. Terror is the reaction of guilt in the face of God's holiness. It's the desire to run away from God in despair. What the Preacher urges upon those involved in worship isn't some kind of terror that drives them away from God but an invitation for them to stand in fear of God.

To fear God is to live in adoration of Him and His character. It's to realize with shame that though we are created in His image, our sin has tarnished that image. Fearing Him is to recognize the costly way in which the image of God would be restored: by God sending His Son to die in order that we, entering the benefits of His death, may stand before our righteous Judge forgiven. In the cross of the Lord Jesus Christ, all of God's justice is brought to bear, and all of His love is made manifest. When our souls begin to grapple with these realities, then we can join the psalmist in declaring, "With you there is forgiveness, that you may be feared" (Ps. 130:4).

In two or three sentences, summarize the main point of this passage. How does it fit into the broader picture of God's revelation?

Live Out the Book

Ecclesiastes 5:1–7 makes it clear that when we come into the context of worship, our aim is to glorify the Lord, exalting His name. Worship is meant to turn our gaze from the earth upward to heaven, from time to eternity, and from ourselves to God. Therefore, we must guard our steps, watch our mouths, keep our vows, and—most of all—stand in awe.

Still, we know that God is looking not for worshippers who are perfect but for those who are humble and honest before Him. Just as parents adore the little scribbles and drawings their kids make for them, so, too, does God accept whatever we do out of genuine love for Him in Christ.

What about God's character demands that we fear Him (Eccl. 5:7)? How is fearing Him an act of worship?

Would you say that your approach to worship is marked by reverence? If not, what characterizes your worship? Reflect on the ways Ecclesiastes 5:1–7 challenges your view of worship.

How do Christ's words in John 4:23–24 inform how you view worship? In what ways are you obedient to His command on this matter?

♪

Praise and Prayer

USE PSALM 96 FOR PRAISE AND MEDITATION:

Oh sing to the LORD a new song;
  sing to the LORD, all the earth!
Sing to the LORD, bless his name;
  tell of his salvation from day to day.
Declare his glory among the nations,
  his marvelous works among all the peoples!
For great is the LORD, and greatly to be praised;
  he is to be feared above all gods.
For all the gods of the peoples are worthless idols,
  but the LORD made the heavens.
Splendor and majesty are before him;
  strength and beauty are in his sanctuary.

Ascribe to the LORD, O families of the peoples,
  ascribe to the LORD glory and strength!
Ascribe to the LORD the glory due his name;
  bring an offering, and come into his courts!
Worship the LORD in the splendor of holiness;
  tremble before him, all the earth!

Say among the nations, “The LORD reigns!
Yes, the world is established; it shall never be moved;
he will judge the peoples with equity.”

Let the heavens be glad, and let the earth rejoice;
let the sea roar, and all that fills it;
let the field exult, and everything in it!
Then shall all the trees of the forest sing for joy
before the LORD, for he comes,
for he comes to judge the earth.
He will judge the world in righteousness,
and the peoples in his faithfulness.

Praise and Prayer

USE THE TRUTHS LEARNED FOR PERSONAL PRAYER:

- **Repent** of the ways that you have knowingly or unknowingly made light of worship.
- **Confess** to the Lord your sins—deeds left undone that *ought* to have been done and deeds done that *ought not* to have been done.
- **Prayerfully** consider the ways that you can prepare your heart for corporate worship each week.

Further Study

- **Related passages:** Psalm 34:1–3; Romans 12:1–2
- **Related sermon:** "Concerning Worship"
- **Related series:** *What Is True Worship?*

Scan the QR code to find links to the additional resources, or visit tfl.org/ecclesiastes-list.

SESSION SIX

ECCLESIASTES 5:8–6:12

IN SEARCH OF MEANING

"He who loves money will not be satisfied with money, nor he who loves wealth with his income; this also is vanity." **—Ecclesiastes 5:10**

Open the Book

Go to the Lord in prayer, asking Him to help you understand and receive His Word. Then read Ecclesiastes 5:8–6:12.

In a sentence or two, summarize what this passage says. (For this response, focus on understanding what the words themselves communicate. Don't move yet to application.)

What literary features are present in this passage? (Look for repeated words, contrasts, metaphors, questions and answers, illustrations, and references or allusions to other parts of Scripture.)

What lingering questions do you have?

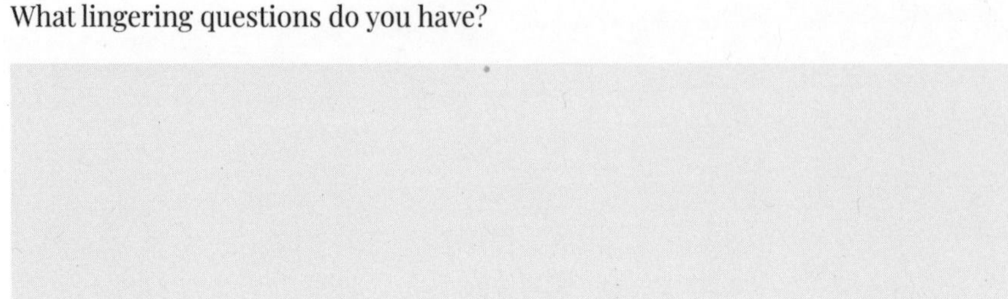

Study the Book

Money is the focus in the second part of Ecclesiastes 5. The Preacher has told us how he wandered down darkened avenues, searching for a meaningful life. There was nowhere he wouldn't go; there was nothing he was unprepared to try. But none of the prospects that held out hope for him delivered on what they promised. As we've considered, the routes to apparent happiness wound up being dead-end streets.

At the same time, the Preacher seems to have had moments that created the impression that he was being haunted by God's shadow. Into his futile experiences came an awareness that God, to whom he'd payed little attention, wasn't far from him at all.

This brings us to Ecclesiastes 5:8, where the Preacher relates his journey down the path of money. He offers us three accompanying insights on this important issue.

Injustice

The Preacher observes in **verses 8–9** that wherever we find money in abundance, we'll also find injustice. It's important to remember, of course, that he is speaking proverbially. In general, though, if we see a poor person being oppressed by the powerful, we shouldn't be surprised—it's a fact of life. (We should, however, be saddened and righteously angry.) Everyone takes orders from those higher up the ladder, and the lower one is on that ladder, the more justice becomes an unaffordable luxury **(v. 8)**. Aware of such realities, we have all the more reason to praise the Lord when we see leaders—whether in business, government, communities, or anywhere else—who are striving for righteous prosperity for all **(v. 9)**.

Indigestion

Wealth also produces indigestion: "He who loves money will not be satisfied with money, nor he who loves wealth with his income; this also is vanity" **(v. 10)**. In other words, money is an insatiable appetite. We can never have enough. Truth be told, if there's anything worse than the excess that money brings, it's the emptiness it leaves.

The Preacher aims to expose the real issue in our hearts: not our desire for more money but our seeking a sense of inward fulfillment that we think can be *found* in more money. To make matters worse, the more money we have, the more people there will be who want our money **(v. 11)**! Not surprisingly, the Preacher concludes in **verse 12** that affluence plus indulgence equals restlessness. Clearly, wealth isn't all that it promises to be.

Insignificance

Along with injustice and indigestion, money brings with it insignificance in **verses 13–15**. "Naked in, naked out"—this is the spirit of the Preacher's words in **verse 14**. We didn't come down the birth canal wearing sneakers or holding shopping bags, nor can we take those things with us when we die **(v. 15)**. Unless we invest in heaven's bank, the Bible teaches, life is marked by debt and destruction (Matt. 6:19–21).

In fact, that's the whole emphasis of **chapter 6**. The entire chapter is a graphic illustration of the meaninglessness of this "grievous evil." In short (echoing his bleak words in chapter 4), the Preacher asserts that it is better to be a stillborn than a wealthy man with a hundred children in his old age but with no satisfaction in life **(vv. 1–3)**.

Compounding this astounding claim, the Preacher shows in **verses 10–12** that the rat race of life in itself makes no sense at all. To live "under the sun"—apart from God with no absolute values for which to live and no practical certainties for which to plan—is like being a soccer player who runs up and down a field without goals, lines, or a penalty spot. Life lived in this manner is a complete waste of time—and no amount of money can fix it.

In two or three sentences, summarize the main point of this passage. How does it fit into the broader picture of God's revelation?

Live Out the Book

The desire for money is something with which we can all identify, whether we have a lot or a little. Money can give us a sense of power and control over our lives. But often, just when we think we've got it under control, life catches us off guard, thwarting our plans and exposing the fact that we control very little. In these moments, we may see the shadow of God's hand, as it were, knocking on the door of our souls, as it did the Preacher's.

Though we try to escape God's creating and sustaining power by pursuing futile loves such as money, we'd do well to recognize that there isn't an exit on life's freeway that, when taken, allows us to escape from God's hand at all (Ps. 139:7–12). While money itself isn't evil, seeking inward fulfillment from anything apart from God most certainly is.

What can we discern from Ecclesiastes 5 about what God requires of us as it pertains to money, stewardship, and wealth?

This portion of Ecclesiastes exposes several problems that can accompany money. What are some of your fears and anxieties when it comes to money? How may you bring God's Word to bear on those issues?

What attitudes or presuppositions about money do you need to adjust to more fully honor Jesus in this area of your life?

Praise and Prayer

USE PSALM 112 FOR PRAISE AND MEDITATION:

Praise the LORD!
Blessed is the man who fears the LORD,
who greatly delights in his commandments!
His offspring will be mighty in the land;
the generation of the upright will be blessed.
Wealth and riches are in his house,
and his righteousness endures forever.
Light dawns in the darkness for the upright;
he is gracious, merciful, and righteous.
It is well with the man who deals generously and lends;
who conducts his affairs with justice.
For the righteous will never be moved;
he will be remembered forever.
He is not afraid of bad news;
his heart is firm, trusting in the LORD.
His heart is steady; he will not be afraid,
until he looks in triumph on his adversaries.
He has distributed freely; he has given to the poor;
his righteousness endures forever;
his horn is exalted in honor.
The wicked man sees it and is angry;
he gnashes his teeth and melts away;
the desire of the wicked will perish!

Praise and Prayer

USE THE TRUTHS LEARNED FOR PERSONAL PRAYER:

- **Confess** your sins of greed, discontentment, and worry as they relate to money.
- **Thank** God for His provision.
- **Ask** the Lord to show you how you can use your finances for His glory.
- **Ask** Christ to give you contentment with what He has given you, physically and spiritually.

Further Study

- **Related passages:** Matthew 6:19–24; 1 Timothy 6:6–10
- **Related sermon:** "In Search of Meaning"
- **Related article:** "Following Jesus Means Trusting the Father's Provision"

Scan the QR code to find links to the additional resources, or visit tfl.org/ecclesiastes-list.

SESSION SEVEN

ECCLESIASTES 7

WISDOM VS. FOLLY

*"See, this alone I found, that God made man upright, but they have sought out many schemes." —**Ecclesiastes 7:29***

Open the Book

Go to the Lord in prayer, asking Him to help you understand and receive His Word. Then read Ecclesiastes 7.

In a sentence or two, summarize what this passage says. (For this response, focus on understanding what the words themselves communicate. Don't move yet to application.)

What literary features are present in this passage? (Look for repeated words, contrasts, metaphors, questions and answers, illustrations, and references or allusions to other parts of Scripture.)

What lingering questions do you have?

Study the Book

Ecclesiastes 7 contrasts wise living with foolish living. This chapter's structure is a lot like what we find in the book of Proverbs: a staccato burst of insights that hit us from all angles, coalescing around a few central themes.

The Value of a Good Name

Verse 1 begins, "A good name is better than precious ointment." For Ecclesiastes's first readers, "precious ointment" (or what we may today call fine perfume) would have been a luxury few could have afforded. It was an indication of wealth; even today, we don't usually find poverty-stricken people spending hundreds of dollars on half-ounce bottles of expensive fragrances! What the Preacher means, then, is that it's better to pass down a legacy of a good name than to enjoy the luxuries of finer things. A good name is far better than riches. It's a matter of honor.

Sorrow, Suffering, and Spiritual Formation

The next five verses **(vv. 2–6)** call us to face several hard facts. Life is difficult, they remind us—and one day, for all of us, it will end. Only when we reckon with this matter will we realize it's better to mourn with the sensible than feast with fools **(v. 2)**. Similarly, facing the facts of hardship and death, we can say with the Preacher, "Sorrow is better than laughter" **(v. 3)**. Comedy is fleeting; tragedy is formative. Charles Spurgeon once said, "Affliction is the best bit of furniture in my house."[3] In other words, life confirms what the Bible conveys: More spiritual progress is made through failure, disappointment, hard times, and tears than will be discovered in success, laughter, easy times, and trivialities. (This, of course, is very countercultural!)

Wisdom in Self-Control

Verses 7–10 stress the importance of exercising self-control. Starting with **verse 7**, we see the importance of self-control in the matters of money, because "a bribe corrupts the heart." In other words, we should be careful not to lose our credibility—our ability to do business with a clean conscience and crystal-clear gaze. We are to be careful also in the snare of unguarded talk, as **verses 8–9** warn. We must not allow our mouths to run ahead of our minds. And we are to guard not only *how* we speak but also *what* we say. (That's **verse 10**.) No one wants to be known as the crabby old fool walking around saying, "Man, I miss the good old days!" Taking a mental holiday dreaming about the past to avoid putting our shoulder to the plow in the present is a folly to avoid at all costs.

Wisdom in Trust

In **verses 11–12**, the Preacher simply highlights the value of wisdom against life's risks, describing wisdom as "protection" for our lives **(v. 12)**. The next verse is a call simply for us to *trust*. Life is neither the product of blind fate nor a series of random chance occurrences; God is over all and in control of all—everything is "the work of God" **(v. 13)**.

The advice that follows in **verse 14** is straightforward: "In the day of prosperity be joyful, and in the day of adversity consider: God has made the one as well as the other, so that man may not find out anything that will be after him." God is in control of the rain and the clouds as much as He is of the sun and the beauty. He's sovereign over the good days and the bad days. The Preacher urges his readers to consider these truths and trust in God.

---

[3] C. H. Spurgeon, "The Trial of Your Faith," *The Metropolitan Tabernacle Pulpit* 34, no. 2055, 657.

The Righteous and the Wicked

In **verses 15–22**, the Preacher's focus then shifts to the distinction between righteous and wicked living. Contrary to popular notions of health, wealth, and happiness, the idea that the righteous automatically prosper and the wicked automatically suffer simply isn't true **(v. 15)**. Though in the end God will right all wrongs, our experience in the meantime isn't so black-and-white. The righteous sometimes perish in their uprightness, while the wicked prolong their lives in their evil.

How do we deal with this paradox? The Preacher offers surprising counsel in **verse 16**: "Be not overly righteous, and do not make yourself too wise." We shouldn't take this as an encouragement to sin! Rather, the Preacher is warning against a spiritual intensity pushed too far. We ought to avoid the heart posture of the Pharisees in Jesus' day, who condemned our Lord for neglecting their extrabiblical additions to God's law.

So we're not to be overly righteous, on the one hand. On the other, though, he warns us, "Be not overly wicked" **(v. 17)**. How, then, do we resolve this tension? Do we walk the tightrope between the two extremes? No, the answer is given in **verse 18**: "The one who fears God shall come out from both of them." We're to *fear* God, living in a way that asks of every thought and deed, "Will the Lord approve of and be honored by this?"

The Preacher closes this section by revisiting a familiar theme, commending wisdom amid the wickedness of our world **(vv. 19–22)**.

The Folly of Sinfulness

Verses 23–29 then remind us not only of the Preacher's ongoing search but also of humanity's fallen condition. He concludes, "See, this alone I found, that God made man upright, but they have sought out many schemes" **(v. 29)**. Though the Preacher tried his best to let wisdom be his guide—to live uprightly—he was undone in the end by his own plans. Foolishness, when the Bible speaks about it, has to do not with mental faculty but with moral rebellion. All of our folly is found in our sinfulness, our disobedience to and rebellion against the will of our Creator—the one who loves us, sustains us, and will one day assess us. Our sinful folly brings condemnation before our holy God, for He must punish sin.

In two or three sentences, summarize the main point of this passage. How does it fit into the broader picture of God's revelation?

Live Out the Book

We can read the Preacher's insight in **verse 29** as an invitation to believe the Gospel. Like the Preacher, many of us have embarked on foolish journeys down dead-end streets. But we don't have to feel alienated or condemned, for the Lord Jesus Christ, God's Son, came to be the answer to our dilemma. God has provided the way of salvation in the cross of Christ. There all His love and justice are expressed. There He meets our needs precisely. And in the empty tomb we find hope for new, eternal life!

When we turn to Christ in our sinfulness and in our emptiness, we receive His fullness and forgiveness. Only then can we turn away from sin—from our folly—and start out on a new path.

What benefit is there to considering the work of God, as Ecclesiastes 7:13 prompts us to do? In what sense does God's work in creation reveal truth about His character?

What is the difference between soberly reflecting on the past and wishing to relive it (Eccl. 7:10)? What dangers does the latter pose? What wisdom might the former provide?

How does the path of salvation prove to be a better way than the dead-end pursuits this world offers?

♪

Praise and Prayer

USE THIS EXCERPT FROM CHARLES SPURGEON'S SERMON ON ECCLESIASTES 7 FOR PRAISE AND MEDITATION:

Consider it spiritually, and, dear brethren, what is a good name? A good name is a name that is written in the Lamb's book of life, and that is better than the sweetest of all ointments. Oh, that I may find my name recorded in some corner of the page among the sinners saved by grace. The very thought of that has a savour in it which no earthly delicacy can rival. Oh, how blessed to be among the chosen of God, the redeemed of Christ Jesus, beloved of the Father from before the foundation of the world. ... If you could see your name written on the palms of his hands you would say, " ... Though it is a name that has been ridiculed, though it is a name that has been bandied about and kicked like a football through the world, yet it is a blessed name, for it is written on the palms of Jesus' hands." It is so if we are the Lord's own people, and are walking the walk of faith. Jesus says, "I have graven thee upon the palms of my hands." That is a good name which is recorded in the Lamb's book of life, and engraved upon the breastplate of the Saviour. Do you not think so?[4]

[4] C. H. Spurgeon, "The Believer's Deathday Better Than His Birthday," *The Metropolitan Tabernacle Pulpit* 27, no. 1588, 146.

Praise and Prayer

USE THE TRUTHS LEARNED FOR PERSONAL PRAYER:

- **Praise** God for sending His Son to be "the way, and the truth, and the life" (John 14:6) for you.
- **Pray** that Jesus' name, not your own, would be glorified through you.
- **Ask** the Lord to sanctify you through the failures, disappointments, and trials you endure.
- **Repent** of your tendency to fear the wrong things. **Ask** God to spur within you a proper fear of Him.

Further Study

- **Related passages:** Galatians 5:22–23; 2 Timothy 3:1–5
- **Related devotions:** "Death Is but a Doorway" and "God's Wisdom"

Scan the QR code to find links to the additional resources, or visit tfl.org/ecclesiastes-list.

SESSION EIGHT

ECCLESIASTES 8–9

THE CASE AGAINST SELF-SUFFICIENCY

"This is an evil in all that is done under the sun, that the same event happens to all. Also, the hearts of the children of man are full of evil, and madness is in their hearts while they live, and after that they go to the dead." **—Ecclesiastes 9:3**

Open the Book

Go to the Lord in prayer, asking Him to help you understand and receive His Word. Then read Ecclesiastes 8–9.

In a sentence or two, summarize what this passage says. (For this response, focus on understanding what the words themselves communicate. Don't move yet to application.)

What literary features are present in this passage? (Look for repeated words, contrasts, metaphors, questions and answers, illustrations, and references or allusions to other parts of Scripture.)

What lingering questions do you have?

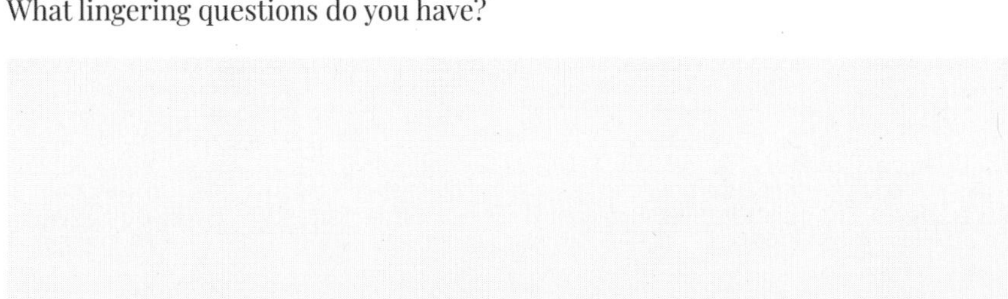

Study the Book

In Ecclesiastes 8–9, the Preacher wrestles with what we may call the riddle of life. He continues to discover that apart from God, our lives are very much like Russian nesting dolls: Just when we think we've seen all there is, we open it again to be confronted with another layer. We're all searching for meaning, trying to make sense of our existence—and the more we consider our days as they ebb and flow, the more questions about them we discover. These two chapters underscore four truths for navigating life's enigmas.

Life Is Unfair

The first truth is that life is as unfair as it is unmanageable. The Preacher has already observed the injustice of the righteous perishing and the wicked prospering **(Eccl. 7:15)**. This concept resurfaces in **8:14**, where he notes how the wicked often receive the righteous person's dues and vice versa. The innocent fall prey to violence. The greedy cheat and end up living lives of ease and luxury. Life is unfair, and the examples are endless—which is exactly his point.

People Are Unreliable

Second, just as life is unfair, so people often prove unreliable. For most of us, our lives are all about people—yet as we move through our days, we discover that relationships, no matter how affirming or affectionate, cannot unscramble for us the vastness of the human dilemma. The Preacher tells a parable to this effect in **9:13–15**. He describes a small city besieged by a powerful king—but in this city was a poor, wise man who "by his wisdom delivered the city." And what did this deliverer get in return for his heroism? "No one remembered that poor man" **(v. 15)**. The parable conveys a sobering truth: We can't afford to count on anything as fleeting as public gratitude or acclaim to make sense of our lives.

The Future Is Unpredictable

Along the road of life's enigmas, the Preacher also asserts that the future is unpredictable: Man "does not know what is to be, for who can tell him how it will be?" **(8:7)**. No one knows what lies ahead. The Preacher repeats similar observations in **9:1** and **9:11**, wanting us to see that from our perspective "under the sun," there's neither rhyme nor reason to history's events. In a worldview that denies the existence of a personal creator God, we can find no ultimately satisfying answer to the questions "Why did this happen?" and "Why have I experienced this?"

Many in our day, in their contemporary sophistication, choose to turn their backs on God. They believe in time, chance, Mother Nature, or perhaps even a "god" of their own imagination, but not in the Almighty God. We live at a time when God is naturalized and nature is deified, when God is dethroned (in heart and mind) and nature is enthroned. Under this perspective and a whole host of other worldviews, individuals deny the one who has made them for the express purpose of knowing Him, instead taking their chances on an unpredictable future.

Death Is Unavoidable

Finally, though life is unfair, people are unreliable, and the future is unpredictable, one thing is certain: Death is unavoidable. This reality looms large over **Ecclesiastes 9:1–10**. Without God, this life is the best there is.

But for those of us with true knowledge of God in our worldview, we may make the best of our days **(vv. 7–10)** with the confidence that there is more to come. We can eat, drink, and enjoy relationships, and we can do so with joy, having come to terms with the fact that we will one day die to be raised again to new life. Avoiding the fact of death altogether doesn't change its unavoidable nature **(v. 5)**. It *is* sobering—but it can also be tremendously freeing.

In two or three sentences, summarize the main point of this passage. How does it fit into the broader picture of God's revelation?

Live Out the Book

Life is unfair, people are unreliable, the future is unpredictable, and death is unavoidable. Is that it? Not quite, according to the insight in **9:3**: "Also, the hearts of the children of man are full of evil, and madness is in their hearts while they live, and after that they go to the dead." We have developed a deep-seated flaw, rendering us unable to think clearly about God and our relation to Him. The cause for our frustration amid the riddle of life is our neglecting to consider the weight of our sin. We don't operate in a moral vacuum. Scripture teaches, rather, that we've all gone astray, our hearts are crooked, and sin pervades how we think and feel about everything. From birth, sin enfolds our minds, causing us to think wrongly.

Yet the Bible shines into our darkness and grants, by God's grace, illumination. God reveals that we were made for Him and will remain forever dissatisfied until we know Him. We can know Him personally in His Son, who, on the cross, experienced death so that we might experience life.

The fact of an unpredictable future should lead us to consider God's character. What aspects of God's character might be especially comforting in light of this truth?

How does knowing that your "chief end is to glorify God, and to enjoy Him forever"[5] help to answer life's riddles as discussed in Ecclesiastes 8–9?

Though the world is filled with injustice and frustration now, Christ's future kingdom will not be that way. What promises of Christ might you lay hold of for encouragement as you navigate life this side of eternity?

[5] The Westminster Shorter Catechism, Q. 1.

♪

Praise and Prayer

USE THE FOLLOWING HYMN EXCERPT FOR PRAISE AND MEDITATION:

E'er since by faith I saw the stream
Thy flowing wounds supply,
Redeeming love has been my theme
And shall be till I die,
And shall be till I die,
And shall be till I die;
Redeeming love has been my theme
And shall be till I die.

When this poor lisping, stamm'ring tongue
Lies silent in the grave,
Then in a nobler, sweeter song
I'll sing Thy pow'r to save,
I'll sing Thy pow'r to save,
I'll sing Thy pow'r to save;
Then in a nobler, sweeter song
I'll sing Thy pow'r to save.

"There Is a Fountain Filled with Blood"
by William Cowper

Praise and Prayer

USE THE TRUTHS LEARNED FOR PERSONAL PRAYER:

- **Ask** the Lord to erode your self-reliance and increase your dependence on Him.
- **Ask** the Holy Spirit to grant you a heart of wisdom, enabling you to live to Christ's glory in light of your eventual death.
- **Thank** God for the good gifts He has given you. **Confess** any sins as they pertain to idolatry or poor stewardship.

Further Study

- **Related passages:** 2 Corinthians 12:9–10; Revelation 3:5
- **Related sermon:** "The Case Against Self-Sufficiency"
- **Related article:** "Abiding in Christ in a World of Self-Love"

Scan the QR code to find links to the additional resources, or visit tfl.org/ecclesiastes-list.

SESSION NINE

ECCLESIASTES 10

DEAD FLIES AND LITTLE BIRDS

*"Dead flies make the perfumer's ointment give off a stench; so a little folly outweighs wisdom and honor." —**Ecclesiastes 10:1***

Open the Book

Go to the Lord in prayer, asking Him to help you understand and receive His Word. Then read Ecclesiastes 10.

In a sentence or two, summarize what this passage says. (For this response, focus on understanding what the words themselves communicate. Don't move yet to application.)

What literary features are present in this passage? (Look for repeated words, contrasts, metaphors, questions and answers, illustrations, and references or allusions to other parts of Scripture.)

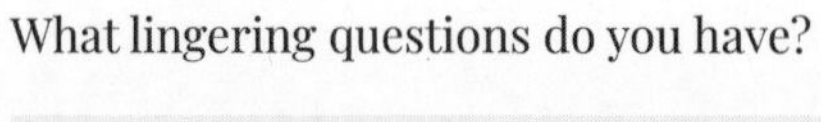

What lingering questions do you have?

Study the Book

Similarly to chapter 7, Ecclesiastes 10 provides us with a series of proverbial statements akin in style to those in the book of Proverbs. Throughout this chapter, the Preacher describes the various places where he has found folly, urging us to resist folly and instead embrace wisdom.

Folly on the Street

In **verses 1–4**, the Preacher describes folly as we find it on the street, or at ground level. The opening statement reads, “Dead flies make the perfumer’s ointment give off a stench; so a little folly outweighs wisdom and honor” **(v. 1)**. In perfume making, one small fly could spoil the whole fragrance. Similarly, it doesn’t take much folly to spoil one’s wisdom and honor. A person can build a strong reputation for decades only to ruin it in a moment of carelessness. One foolish impulse may irreparably spoil something beautiful. And when we do err in this way, **verse 2** adds, it’s ultimately an issue of our hearts. Our hearts can lead us aright or astray, depending on their spiritual condition.

This kind of foolishness isn’t easily disguised. The Preacher paints a comical picture to illustrate his point in **verse 3**: “When the fool walks on the road … he says to everyone that he is a fool.” Like a drunk person walking the streets, he shows no restraint, foolishly babbling on to those around them.

Observing more folly at ground level, the Preacher warns of how a foolish boss can make his employee rush out of an opportunity **(v. 4)**. It’s better to respond calmly than meet him at his level, so to speak. Patience and folly seldom hold hands as they walk down the street.

Folly in High Places

From folly on the street, the Preacher moves next to consider folly in high places. Folly knows no class distinctions, according to **verses 5–7**. This is hardly surprising; there have been fools in government consistently throughout history, and when we have the leadership described in **verse 5**, then the upheavals of **verses 6–7** are only to be expected. When what's natural, sensible, and orderly is in place, wisdom will thrive—but the inverse is also true: When unnatural, unsensible, and disorderly practices pervade leadership, folly will expand.

The danger is that folly does not live in high places alone but bleeds down into the very structure of society, as **verses 16–17** illustrate. Which is better: the ruler without wisdom **(v. 16)** or the ruler surrounded by those with self-control **(v. 17)**? Certainly, wisdom in high places is better than folly.

Folly at Work

The third place in which the Preacher observes folly is in the workplace, in **verses 8–11** and **verse 15**. He makes the point that a little preparation, rather than more perspiration, will be met with far greater success. **Verse 10** illustrates the point, reminding us that if a man's ax is dull and unsharpened, he will have to work significantly harder only to get a little return on his effort. Sharpening the ax, wisdom would dictate, goes a long way in yielding a good return. "Wisdom helps one to succeed" **(v. 10)**; but the fool says, "I don't want to take the time to sharpen the ax. Give me the thing, and let me get at it!"

Folly delays unduly when it's time to proceed; it blisters ahead when it should wait. The work of a fool, according to **verse 15**, is absolute weariness to him.

Folly in Words

Finally, the Preacher locates folly in speech: "The words of a wise man's mouth win him favor, but the lips of a fool consume him" **(v. 12)**. He clearly believes that talk isn't cheap, nor is it to be taken lightly. It's no surprise when, as **verse 13** describes, the fool's words end up as "evil madness." The fool believes he has no one to whom he's accountable, so his words are a continual slide into ever-deepening experiences of madness and wickedness. In this sense, the fool "multiplies words" **(v. 14)**.

Of course, we all have foolish moments. But what's described here is something far more essential. It's a description of the ungodly, whose way of speaking reveals their condition and, ultimately, their destiny.

In Matthew 12:34, Jesus rebukes the Pharisees with these words: "You brood of vipers! How can you speak good, when you are evil? For out of the abundance of the heart the mouth speaks." Ultimately, the fool's problem is in his or her heart. The heart transformed by the wisdom of God will reveal itself in how a person speaks. But the heart that remains unchanged will equally reveal itself by its language. For that reason **verse 20** concludes, "Even in your thoughts, do not curse the king, nor in your bedroom curse the rich, for a bird of the air will carry your voice, or some winged creature tell the matter." The Preacher urges us to be careful, considering how we speak.

In two or three sentences, summarize the main point of this passage. How does it fit into the broader picture of God's revelation?

Live Out the Book

Folly can be observed in the streets, in high places, in the workplace, and in our words. But Scripture speaks of another location for folly: *in the end*. In short, being a fool in this life means facing the next life unprepared. If we don't deal with our folly now, we won't have the chance to do so once we die. Should we choose to live in our folly apart from God today, we'll die in it, without opportunity for reparation, forgiveness, or change.

We must call it what it is: Folly is sin, because it's disobedience to and rebellion against God's will. But the message of the Gospel is this: By His death, Jesus has made provision for our sins and enables us to be reconciled to God. As 1 Corinthians 1:18 says, "The word of the cross is folly to those who are perishing, but to us who are being saved it is the power of God." The plea of Scripture is plain, urging us to turn from folly to truth.

How does the folly spoken of in Ecclesiastes 10 reveal our need for God's wisdom?

God's Word commends a standard of wisdom different from that of the world. In what ways might you be following the world's wisdom rather than God's? How can you correct that pattern?

While the Preacher observed folly in high places, our Lord calls us to honor and pray for those in positions of leadership (Matt. 22:15–22; 1 Tim. 2:1–4). What are some ways that you could pray for wisdom for those in authority?

♪

Praise and Prayer

USE PSALM 111 FOR PRAISE AND MEDITATION:

Praise the LORD!
I will give thanks to the LORD with my whole heart,
  in the company of the upright, in the congregation.
Great are the works of the LORD,
  studied by all who delight in them.
Full of splendor and majesty is his work,
  and his righteousness endures forever.
He has caused his wondrous works to be remembered;
  the LORD is gracious and merciful.
He provides food for those who fear him;
  he remembers his covenant forever.
He has shown his people the power of his works,
  in giving them the inheritance of the nations.
The works of his hands are faithful and just;
  all his precepts are trustworthy;
they are established forever and ever,
  to be performed with faithfulness and uprightness.
He sent redemption to his people;
  he has commanded his covenant forever.
  Holy and awesome is his name!
The fear of the LORD is the beginning of wisdom;
  all those who practice it have a good understanding.
  His praise endures forever!

Praise and Prayer

USE THE TRUTHS LEARNED FOR PERSONAL PRAYER:

- **Ask** God for wisdom, that you may see areas of folly in your life.
- **Repent** of your tendency to act foolishly rather than obey God's will.
- **Thank** the Father for sending His Son to exemplify and embody true wisdom.

Further Study

- **Related passages:** Matthew 12:34–37; 1 Corinthians 1:18–21
- **Related sermon:** "Dead Flies and Little Birds"
- **Related devotions:** "Upstarts and the Truly Great" and "Everyday Dangers" by Charles Spurgeon

Scan the QR code to find links to the additional resources, or visit tfl.org/ecclesiastes-list.

SESSION TEN

ECCLESIASTES 11

CELEBRATE LIFE!

"Rejoice, O young man, in your youth, and let your heart cheer you in the days of your youth. Walk in the ways of your heart and the sight of your eyes. But know that for all these things God will bring you into judgment." **—Ecclesiastes 11:9**

Open the Book

Go to the Lord in prayer, asking Him to help you understand and receive His Word. Then read Ecclesiastes 11.

In a sentence or two, summarize what this passage says. (For this response, focus on understanding what the words themselves communicate. Don't move yet to application.)

What literary features are present in this passage? (Look for repeated words, contrasts, metaphors, questions and answers, illustrations, and references or allusions to other parts of Scripture.)

What lingering questions do you have?

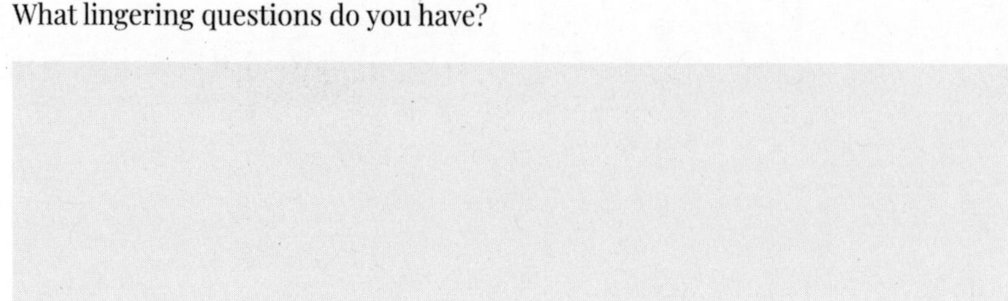

Study the Book

Ecclesiastes 11 summons the reader to celebrate life. If chapter 10 issued a cautionary note to be sensible, then chapter 11 is a call to be bold. Organizing his thoughts as another string of staccato exhortations, the Preacher in this section invites us to seize the moment and enjoy God's blessings all our days.

Go for It! Diversify! Stick with It!

Verse 1 begins with a puzzling metaphor: "Cast your bread upon the waters, for you will find it after many days." We may summarize this curious piece of advice simply with the words *Go for it!* This verse is a reminder of what God is able to do. When we're prepared to take whatever God has entrusted to us—life, talent, resources, time—and throw it out onto the water of life, Scripture promises that it will return to us according to God's design. We see this principle in Isaiah 55:10–11 pertaining specifically to God's Word: It never returns to Him empty but always accomplishes its purpose. Conversely, buried treasure brings strong condemnation (Matt. 25:14–30).

In **verse 2** we find a second directive. The Preacher advises us, in essence, to diversify our assets. Because we never know which venture we embark upon will work, we must be careful not to put all of our eggs in one basket, instead seizing with enthusiasm the variety of opportunities before us.

A third exhortation appears in **verse 6**, which we might paraphrase as *Stick with it!* The Preacher mentions "morning" and "evening"—that is, there are different stages in life, and we ought to be prepared to keep going, to continue taking initiative to think imaginatively and creatively in every season. Indeed, the kind of person we'll be in our old age is largely determined by the kind of person we are now. "Launch out in new directions," the Preacher says, "and when you meet adversity, don't give up."

Don't Wait for Ideal Conditions

The above three statements from the Preacher come with an important qualifier in **verses 3–5**: *Don't wait for ideal conditions.* Life's inevitable challenges—the clouds full of rain or a falling tree—shouldn't thwart our initiative or endeavor **(v. 3)**. Many obstacles are unavoidable and beyond our control. We shouldn't stay inside just because it's raining. Instead, we should get an umbrella or raincoat and *go*!

Similarly, **verse 4** urges us not to get caught up in uncertainties. The farmer who waits on the wind to plant his seed will never reap a harvest. It's folly to linger too long in doubt, for life is packed with mysterious matters that we'll never fully understand **(v. 5)**. Wisdom would have us move forward, not allowing the unknown and unknowable to paralyze us.

Enjoy! Be Happy! Relax!

Three more encouragements emerge from the chapter. The first comes in **verses 7–8**: "Light is sweet, and it is pleasant for the eyes to see the sun" **(v. 7)**. In other words: *Enjoy!* We should delight in the sunlight for however long God would have us live. "All that comes is vanity," the Preacher acknowledges **(v. 8)**; our enjoyment is not unending but temporary, and by themselves, temporal blessings like sunlight can never ultimately satisfy. But the anticipation of our heavenly dwelling shines down, as it were, onto our earthly pilgrimage. We will do well to enjoy it.

Verse 9 then urges us, *Be happy!* The Preacher offers a dimension of freedom that ought to allure us, a freedom that has a "Well done, good and faithful servant" for which to strive (Matt. 25:23). Of course, remove God from our perspective, and the pursuit of happiness is swallowed up by triviality. But of all people on earth, the believer ought to lead the world in enjoying life and experiencing happiness. Along the continuum of life, the believer acknowledges the wonder of what God provides, which ought to move us to be happy.

The third and final exhortation is *Relax!* **Verse 10** concludes, "Remove vexation from your heart, and put away pain from your body, for youth and the dawn of life are vanity." While we shouldn't be careless, we ought to be carefree. That doesn't mean we should embrace indifference or irresponsibility—but just as dreading the loss of our youth will spoil its God-intended experience, similarly, trying to perpetuate it will wind up making us look foolish. So we should relax, removing the vexation from our hearts.

Don't Forget the Final Exam

Verse 9 includes a final qualifying statement: "Walk in the ways of your heart and the sight of your eyes. But know that for all these things God will bring you into judgment." In other words, we are to enjoy, be happy, and relax—but not foolishly. In the end, God will bring us into judgment (Matt. 12:36).

In two or three sentences, summarize the main point of this passage. How does it fit into the broader picture of God's revelation?

Live Out the Book

Ecclesiastes 11 tells us that we are to enjoy life, but not foolishly. Folly is sin. Yet while believers don't rejoice in their sin, we *do* still sin. We haven't perfectly kept God's commandments. Therefore, we have a predicament! How, then, should we prepare to meet God on that final day of judgment **(Eccl. 11:9)**? By trusting in Christ's work on our behalf. Jesus alone has kept the law perfectly, and the good news of the Gospel is that on the cross, He has borne the punishment finally so that we may find in Him the life that is really life.

How does knowing God enable us to truly celebrate life? Is it possible to enjoy life apart from knowing God? Why or why not?

What bearing does the fact of God's future, final judgment have on how you live today?

How can you better lay hold of the life that you have in the Lord Jesus Christ (e.g., sins to repent of, promises to believe, changes to make)?

♪

Praise and Prayer

USE THIS EXCERPT FROM CHARLES SPURGEON'S SERMON ON ECCLESIASTES 11 FOR PRAISE AND MEDITATION:

We are guilty … of *unbelief*, if we cannot sow because of the wind. Who manages the wind? You distrust him who is Lord of north, and south, and east, and west. If you cannot reap because of a cloud, you doubt him who makes the clouds, to whom the clouds are the dust of his feet. Where is your faith? Where is your faith? "Ah!" says one, "I can serve God when I am helped, when I am moved, when I can see a hope of success." That is poor service, service devoid of faith. May I not say of it, "Without faith it is impossible to please God"? Just in proportion to the quantity of faith that there is in what we do, in that proportion will it be acceptable with God. Observing of winds and clouds is unbelief. We may call it prudence; but unbelief is its true name.[6]

[6] C. H. Spurgeon, "Sowing in the Wind; Reaping Under Clouds," *The Metropolitan Tabernacle Pulpit* 38, no. 2264, 329–30.

Praise and Prayer

USE THE TRUTHS LEARNED FOR PERSONAL PRAYER:

- **Ask** God to grant you a heart that enjoys life and its gifts.
- **Reflect** on areas of your life that are marked more by drudgery than enjoyment, bringing them to the Lord in prayer.
- **Pray** for diligence in your calling—as a spouse, parent, employee, friend, etc.

Further Study

- **Related passages:** Matthew 25:14–30; Ephesians 5:15–17
- **Related sermon:** "Celebrate Life!"
- **Related article:** "Four Core Truths About the Second Coming of Christ"

Scan the QR code to find links to the additional resources, or visit tfl.org/ecclesiastes-list.

SESSION ELEVEN

ECCLESIASTES 12:1–8

"REMEMBER YOUR CREATOR"

"Remember also your Creator in the days of your youth, before the evil days come and the years draw near of which you will say, 'I have no pleasure in them.'" ***—Ecclesiastes 12:1***

Open the Book

Go to the Lord in prayer, asking Him to help you understand and receive His Word. Then read Ecclesiastes 12:1–8.

In a sentence or two, summarize what this passage says. (For this response, focus on understanding what the words themselves communicate. Don't move yet to application.)

What literary features are present in this passage? (Look for repeated words, contrasts, metaphors, questions and answers, illustrations, and references or allusions to other parts of Scripture.)

What lingering questions do you have?

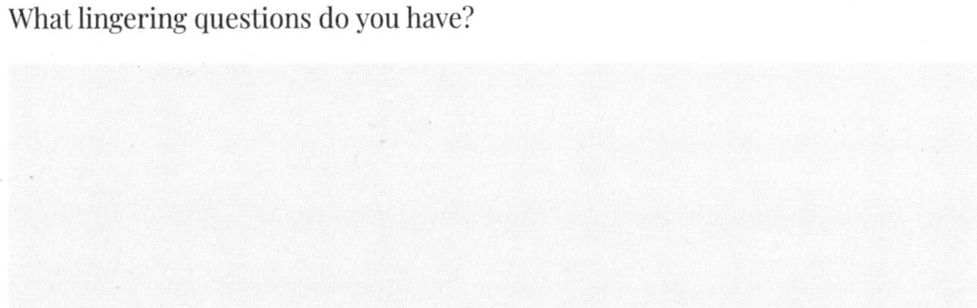

Study the Book

In the first part of Ecclesiastes 12, the Preacher calls his readers to remember their Creator while they're yet young. Turning back from the dead-end streets on which we walk, we ought to remember God while we still have the opportunity. Such remembrance, as we'll discover, isn't perfunctory, theoretical consideration; it's an act of self-denial that trusts wholly in God. Days of trouble, we're promised, *will* come **(v. 1)**—so it's better to remember now than spend eternity with regret. The call to "remember" is the focus of **verses 1–8**.

The Call to Remember

Verse 1 reads like a thesis: "Remember also your Creator in the days of your youth." Why do so now? Because, as we've seen throughout Ecclesiastes by this point, the springtime of life will inevitably be swallowed up by winter. A chill eventually settles over life, as **verse 2** illustrates; the clouds roll in, turning daylight into gloom. It's a somber picture depicting the fading not only of our physical powers but also our mental faculties—a picture of the general desolation of old age. We ought to remember our Creator while we still have the capacity to do so.

The Years Draw Near

In **verses 3–5**, the Preacher uses poetic language to expound on "the evil days" spoken of in **verse 1**. His words evoke thoughts of decay—a foretaste of every person's future. As we age, our arms shake, our legs lose their strength, and our bodies wear down **(v. 3)**. Before we know it, we're shut in. The ladder seems a lot taller than it was; the streets appear fuller than they were in our youth. Like the almond tree blossoms, our hair changes color. We look like grasshoppers dragging ourselves along, our desire for physical intimacy no longer stirred **(vv. 4–5)**. This is striking imagery of a man heading toward his "eternal home" **(v. 5)**. Before such days come, we should look to God and recall our need for Him.

Remember Your Creator Before You Die

With the subject of death in view, **verse 6** eloquently depicts life's beauty and fragility through a series of related metaphors. Our lives are held between time and eternity by very tender mechanisms. It only takes a small shift for the cord to sever, for the bowl to shatter, for the pitcher to fall into the spring, and for the wheel that has been used to bring the bucket up from the well to find itself propped up against the stones. The Preacher wants us to see the transience of our most basic acts. Just as there is a first time for every routine task, so there will be a last time.

In light of this, the Preacher says with certainty, "The dust returns to the earth as it was, and the spirit returns to God who gave it" **(v. 7)**. It takes no guesswork: Death is a fact of life.

The Preacher concludes his discourse on death with his familiar refrain: "Vanity of vanities, says the Preacher; all is vanity" **(v. 8)**. He ends up where he began in the book's first chapter. Even death, the Preacher notes, is vanity.

In two or three sentences, summarize the main point of this passage. How does it fit into the broader picture of God's revelation?

Live Out the Book

If we view our lives from the framework of futility—that is, apart from God—then the conclusion in **verse 8** is reasonable. But life's journeys need not end there. God, by His Word, doesn't ask us to take on some grand task or earth-shattering quest. He doesn't require that we start a charity organization, climb Kilimanjaro, or run around the block forty-seven times saying manifold prayers. Instead, He simply pleads that we *remember Him*. He calls us to draw near to Him—the creator God who, in His perfect love and timing, sent His Son to be our Savior—and to do so without delay! As Paul writes in 2 Corinthians 6:2, "Now is the favorable time; behold, now is the day of salvation."

God's eternality, when we contrast it with our impending, inevitable deaths, should remind us of His attributes and character. What else can we learn of God through observing this reality?

How well do your priorities today reflect the fact that death is inevitable? What might you need to rearrange or reprioritize to truly live in light of the end?

As the Preacher invites us to remember our Creator, we would do well to remember the Gospel in particular. What benefit is there to meditating on the good news of Christ's work? How could you do this more often?

♪

Praise and Prayer

USE PSALM 135:1–14 FOR PRAISE AND MEDITATION:

Praise the LORD!
Praise the name of the LORD,
   give praise, O servants of the LORD,
who stand in the house of the LORD,
   in the courts of the house of our God!
Praise the LORD, for the LORD is good;
   sing to his name, for it is pleasant!
For the LORD has chosen Jacob for himself,
   Israel as his own possession.

For I know that the LORD is great,
   and that our LORD is above all gods.
Whatever the LORD pleases, he does,
   in heaven and on earth,
   in the seas and all deeps.
He it is who makes the clouds rise at the end of the earth,
   who makes lightnings for the rain
   and brings forth the wind from his storehouses.

He it was who struck down the firstborn of Egypt,
   both of man and of beast;
who in your midst, O Egypt,
   sent signs and wonders
   against Pharaoh and all his servants;
who struck down many nations
   and killed mighty kings,
Sihon, king of the Amorites,
   and Og, king of Bashan,
   and all the kingdoms of Canaan,
and gave their land as a heritage,
   a heritage to his people Israel.

Your name, O LORD, endures forever,
   your renown, O LORD, throughout all ages.
For the LORD will vindicate his people
   and have compassion on his servants.

Praise and Prayer

USE THE TRUTHS LEARNED FOR PERSONAL PRAYER:

- **Prayerfully reflect** on God's character and work. **Thank** Him for those qualities and deeds.
- **Ask** God to reorient your heart, enabling you to live to His glory in all of life.
- **Confess** any sins of negligence as they relate to remembering God in your day-to-day.

Further Study

- **Related passages:** Psalm 90:10–12; Psalm 137:1–6
- **Related sermons:** "'Remember Your Creator'" and "Following Jesus"

Scan the QR code to find links to the additional resources, or visit tfl.org/ecclesiastes-list.

SESSION TWELVE

ECCLESIASTES 12:9–14

A SURPRISING PUNCH LINE

"The end of the matter; all has been heard. Fear God and keep his commandments, for this is the whole duty of man." **—Ecclesiastes 12:13**

Open the Book

Go to the Lord in prayer, asking Him to help you understand and receive His Word. Then read Ecclesiastes 12:9–14.

In a sentence or two, summarize what this passage says. (For this response, focus on understanding what the words themselves communicate. Don't move yet to application.)

What literary features are present in this passage? (Look for repeated words, contrasts, metaphors, questions and answers, illustrations, and references or allusions to other parts of Scripture.)

What lingering questions do you have?

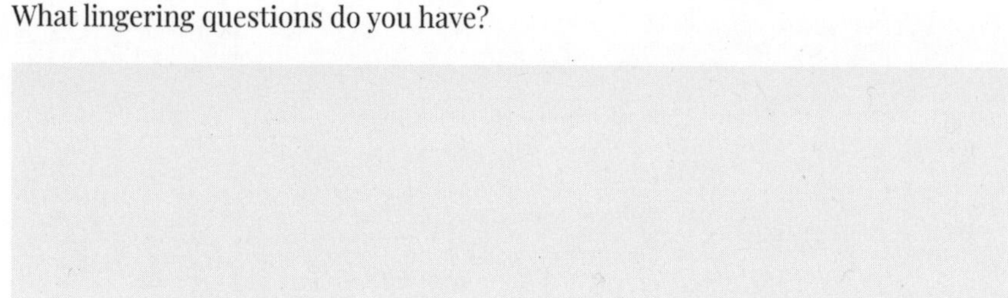

Study the Book

The second half of Ecclesiastes 12 marks the Preacher's conclusion. In the end, having gone down a number of dead-end streets and come face-to-face with life's toughest enigmas, the Preacher concludes that life's every pleasure ultimately mocks us. There's no lasting satisfaction to be found in passing fads and fancies. Even those who have reached the proverbial pot of gold at the end of the rainbow still can't put their hands on it at all.

Some have tried in vain to make sense of the tragedy of life by their own philosophical meanderings. Others have concluded that life isn't tragic at all, just horribly trivial and futile. But the Preacher arrives at a different conclusion—a surprising one, no doubt.

The punch line to the whole book comes in **verse 13**: "The end of the matter; all has been heard. Fear God and keep his commandments, for this is the whole duty of man." This is Ecclesiastes's word to those who are wise.

The Preacher's Efforts Commended

In **verses 9–10**, the Preacher is addressed in the third person, and all his efforts are commended. Where most of Ecclesiastes is written in the first-person voice (from the perspective of "I" and "we"), this brief section introduces an anonymous person to the scene. Essentially, the Preacher is thanked for his instruction of the people. Not only was he wise, but also, with great care, combining felicity with fearlessness, he taught the truth.

The Preacher's Response

The Preacher responds to the commendation in **verses 11–12**. Wise words, he explains, "are like goads"—sharp, pointed sticks used to move cattle to where they need to go. With this picture in mind, he's careful to give credit where credit is due. The wisdom he conveyed to Israel didn't come from himself but from the "one Shepherd" **(v. 11)**.

All wisdom comes from God Himself. The implication in this profound yet simple truth is that we ought always to listen to our Shepherd. He is not far away but nearby; He knows and can *be* known; and He speaks in understandable words, addressing His people with authority and finality.

This reality leads to the warning in **verse 12**: "My son, beware of anything beyond these. Of making many books there is no end, and much study is a weariness of the flesh." Though our world is full of ideas and truth claims, the Preacher reminds us to pour everything we read through the sieve of the God's perfect Word. Every other word of wisdom, acknowledgment, and insight must bow to the truth of Scripture. The Preacher further warns his readers against the weariness that comes from much study—of becoming a lifelong searcher on a self-imposed journey of inquiry without hope of resolution. Such a journey, he cautions, will end in futility.

The End of the Matter

And so we arrive at last at our punch line in **verse 13**, followed by a concluding exhortation in **verse 14**. What is our duty? To "fear God and keep his commandments." For what reason? Because "God will bring every deed into judgment." We dare not succumb to complacency, for nothing goes unnoticed or unassessed. Despite all appearances to the contrary, nothing in our lives is pointless; God actually *is* concerned with the details.

To fear God in the way that the Preacher suggests is not to run from Him in terror. Rather, to fear Him is to trust, love, and know Him. Such reverent fear arises from our discovering the immensity of God's love. It's like the fear of a child for a father—the awareness that even though we disobey and disappoint, still our Father loves us. It fills us with awe. It makes us want to bow down before Him. If He were to cast us out forever, He would be justified—but still He loves us! To recognize the reality of that love and offer our worship and submission in response is what it means to fear God.

We will never know what it is to fear God in this way until we become God's children—and the gateway into His family is by faith in Christ and repentance from sin.

To believe in Jesus is to entrust ourselves to Him. Only then can we truly fear God and keep His commandments, recognizing the pervasive emptiness of our old way of life. The new way, held out to us in Christ, isn't down any of Ecclesiastes's dead-end streets but is on the narrow road that leads to life (Matt. 7:14). At "the end of the matter," apart from God, all *is* vanity—but with God we find forgiveness, fullness, and life everlasting.

In two or three sentences, summarize the main point of this passage. How does it fit into the broader picture of God's revelation?

Live Out the Book

Ecclesiastes raises a question with which we must reckon: Do we love and fear God? If so, then we will find ourselves growing in godliness. And if not, then there's nothing in and of ourselves that can change that.

Maybe that's you. What, then, should you do? The Bible's answer is remarkably simple: "Believe in the Lord Jesus, and you will be saved" (Acts 16:31). As John 1:12 says, "To all who did receive him, who believed in his name, he gave the right to become children of God." Through Jesus, you are more loved and accepted than you ever dared to hope. Jesus paid your debt, bore your punishment, and offers you forgiveness. Entrust yourself to Him. Turn from your sin—from all those dead-end streets under the sun—and turn to Jesus as your Savior.

On the other hand, those who do fear God properly have a question of their own to ask: "Am I keeping His commandments, walking in wisdom and love?" God accepts us in our sinfulness, but then He takes and changes us by His grace and power—and one of the mechanisms He employs to make us increasingly like Him and useful to Him are the commandments of His Word. Our Lord said, "If you love me, you will keep my commandments" (John 14:15). Is your reverence for God evident through the keeping of His commandments by the power Christ provides?

What does keeping God's commandments reveal about our hearts? Why is obedience a crucial part of the Christian life?

How are you doing with fearing God and obeying His commands, really? Reflect on and write about a few areas in which you could grow.

How does the Gospel of Christ both *produce* and *empower* obedience?

♪

Praise and Prayer

USE THE FOLLOWING HYMN FOR PRAISE AND MEDITATION:

Amazing grace (how sweet the sound)
That saved a wretch like me!
I once was lost but now am found,
Was blind, but now I see.

'Twas grace that taught my heart to fear,
And grace my fears relieved;
How precious did that grace appear
The hour I first believed!

Through many dangers, toils, and snares
I have already come;
'Tis grace has brought me safe thus far,
And grace will lead me home.

The Lord has promised good to me;
His word my hope secures;
He will my shield and portion be
As long as life endures.

Yea, when this flesh and heart shall fail
And mortal life shall cease,
I shall possess within the veil
A life of joy and peace.

The earth shall soon dissolve like snow,
The sun forbear to shine;
But God, who called me here below,
Will be forever mine.

When we've been there ten thousand years,
Bright shining as the sun,
We've no less days to sing God's praise
Than when we'd first begun.

"Amazing Grace" by John Newton

Praise and Prayer

USE THE TRUTHS LEARNED FOR PERSONAL PRAYER:

- **Ask** God for a heart that loves Him, trusts Him, and knows Him.
- **Ask** the Lord to soften your heart toward Him, prompting holy fear and joyful obedience.
- **Praise** God for the truths He has purposed to reveal in and through Ecclesiastes.
- **Confess** your dependence on the Lord for the power to obey.

Further Study

- **Related passages:** Matthew 11:28–30; 1 John 5:1–3
- **Related sermon:** "A Surprising Punch Line"
- **Related article:** "What Does Obedience Have to Do with Following Jesus?"

Scan the QR code to find links to the additional resources, or visit tfl.org/ecclesiastes-list.

APPENDIX A

Additional Tips for Groups

Getting Started

Before studying a biblical book in detail, it's important to acquaint oneself with the book as a whole. Here are some ways a group might establish a good foundation for the study prior to beginning the first session:

- Build a "Session Zero" into your meeting calendar, in which you use the first meeting to read the book in its entirety and work through the Introduction content as a group. (Note that this will extend your study an additional week.)

- Have group participants read the book in its entirety *and* the Introduction content prior to the first meeting. Begin with Session One.

A Step-by-Step Meeting Structure for Groups (FOR A 60-MINUTE MEETING)

- Begin with a brief prayer and by reading the passage for the session together. (5 minutes)

- Using the prompts in the **Open the Book** section, have each participant share one key insight from what he or she wrote. (10 minutes)

- Using the **Study the Book** section for reference, work through and discuss the questions provided under **Live Out the Book**. (30 minutes)

- Close by engaging with the **Praise and Prayer** prompts, meditating on the truths from that week's Bible passage. Share praises and prayer points together, and commit to praying for one another throughout the week. (15 minutes)

- Briefly preview the next session, as time allows.

An Open-Ended Meeting Structure for Groups (FOR VARIED MEETING TIMES AND EMPHASES)

Certain groups may want to structure their meetings to fit a specific meeting time or to address particular needs of those in the group. (E.g., some may emphasize the **Praise and Prayer** portion for relationship and accountability, others the **Study** aspect for increased biblical-theological knowledge and reflection.) Here are some guiding principles to consider in tailoring this study guide to best serve your group:

- *Establish good Bible reading habits.* In each meeting, be careful to reinforce the basic pattern of *read, understand, and apply*, with the central passage in view. These three elements should be present to some degree anytime we engage with the Bible.

- *Know your context.* Consider the spiritual maturity of your group and time constraints as you build out your weekly meeting plan.

- *Determine your aim.* Will you place a higher value on relationship building and accountability or biblical study and education? While these study guides are designed to foster both, determining your focus from the outset will help with time allotment and group expectations.

- *Maintain a degree of balance.* For those groups that emphasize relationship, be careful not to neglect study of the text. For those that emphasize study, be careful to incorporate heart-level response and prayer. We need both.

APPENDIX B

Additional Resources

The following resources are highly recommended, and several were helpful in preparing the sermon series *A Study in Ecclesiastes: Chasing the Wind* and, by extension, in the development of this Bible study:

An Exposition of the Book of Ecclesiastes by Charles Bridges

The Pundit's Folly: Chronicles of an Empty Life by Sinclair B. Ferguson

Living Life Backward: How Ecclesiastes Teaches Us to Live in Light of the End by David Gibson

"Ecclesiastes," by G. S. Hendry, in ***The New Bible Commentary*** (edited by Francis Davidson, A. M. Stibbs, and E. F. Kevan)

The Message of Ecclesiastes: A Time to Mourn and a Time to Dance by Derek Kidner

---

To see more resources from Truth For Life and Alistair Begg, visit **truthforlife.org**.

VERSE BY VERSE

Bible Study Series

with

ALISTAIR BEGG

Ecclesiastes: Chasing the Wind

2 Timothy: Guard the Truth

More coming soon!

Other studies from Truth For Life

The Basics of the Christian Faith: A 13-Lesson Survey

Crossing the Barriers: A 12-Lesson Study on Evangelism

My Times Are in Your Hands: A Study in God's Faithfulness in Affliction

Venturing in Faith: A Study on the Life of Abraham

About The Author

Alistair Begg is the Bible teacher on *Truth For Life*, a daily and weekend program that brings the exposition of Scripture to a global audience through radio, podcast, and a wide range of digital and streaming platforms. Since its launch in 1995, *Truth For Life* has featured teaching drawn from Alistair's decades of faithful preaching at Parkside Church, where he served as senior pastor from 1983 until 2025.

Today, Alistair is actively engaged with *Truth For Life* and speaks frequently at conferences throughout the United States and around the world, where he encourages pastors, theology students, and believers and proclaims the Gospel to those who have yet to come to faith in Jesus Christ.

Alistair is the author of several books, including *Name Above All Names*, *Pray Big*, and *Brave by Faith*. His books have been translated into many languages and are read by a global audience.

Alistair began in pastoral ministry in 1975 after graduating from the London School of Theology. Before joining Parkside Church, he served for eight years in Scotland, ministering at Charlotte Chapel in Edinburgh and Hamilton Baptist Church.

Alistair and his wife, Susan, have been married since 1975. They have three grown children and eight grandchildren.